CREAM PUFFS

CREAM PUFFS

and other delicious French pastries

Hannah Miles

photography by Kate Whitaker

RYLAND PETERS & SMALL
LONDON • NEW YORK

Senior Designer Megan Smith
Commissioning Editor
Stephanie Milner
Production Meskerem Berhane
Art Director Leslie Harrington
Editorial Director Julia Charles

Prop Stylist Jo Harris
Food Stylist Lucy McKelvie
Indexer Hilary Bird

Author's acknowledgements
With heartfelt thanks to all at RPS for their
beautiful work on this book and to Kate
Whitaker for stunning photography.
Thanks also to Jo and Lucy for the
wonderful styling. Much love to Heather
and the Girls at HHB agency and to my
friends, family and colleagues at MCL, SFP,
Amphenol and Irvin's Teas who ate all the
cream puffs along the way.

Dedication

To Justina, Sheelah and Damian,
with love xx

First published in 2014
by Ryland Peters & Small
20–21 Jockey's Fields,
London WC1R 4BW
and
519 Broadway, 5th Floor,
New York NY 10012
www.rylandpeters.com

10 9 8 7 6 5 4 3 2 1

Text © Hannah Miles 2014
Design and photographs © Ryland Peters
& Small 2014

ISBN: 978-1-84975-516-0

Printed and bound in China

Note There are certain health risks
associated with whipped cream so always
practice food safety by using fresh cream
before it's expiry date and storing filled
choux buns in an airtight container in the
refrigerator until ready to serve.

CONTENTS

INTRODUCTION

Choux—a buttery pastry that is as light as a feather —makes the most amazing desserts and cakes I know.

Choux paste is one of the best pantry standbys as the main ingredients you need are flour, butter, and eggs. In about half an hour you can have delicate pastries to serve which can be filled with whipped cream or other fillings of your choosing. If you don't have any filling available then why not try the delicate *Choquettes* on page 23, simply topped with sugar nibs or chocolate chips. They are utterly irresistible, particularly straight from the oven.

Initially the process for making choux paste can seem tricky. I have to confess, that when I was learning to bake, for a long time choux paste was my nemesis and on a few occasions it has reduced me to tears. That said, once you have mastered the knack of choux pastry, it is very easy to prepare and can produce amazing desserts very quickly. You just need a good understanding of the texture of the dough and to follow the steps on pages 8–9 carefully.

Once you have prepared your choux paste, it can be piped into a wide variety of shapes. Classic éclairs are oblong choux buns which are often topped with icing. These are traditionally filled with either whipped cream or pastry cream which can be piped in through a small hole into the éclair or you can cut the éclair in half and sandwich it together with cream. Profiteroles are small balls of choux pastry that are generally filled with whipped cream and served with a sauce to pour over. I don't know anyone who can resist a chocolate profiterole! Cream puffs are larger and often served topped with glacé icing. They are generally cut in half

and filled with a wide variety of fillings. *Paris Brest* (named after the Paris to Brest cycle ride) are rings of cream puff in the shape of a bicycle wheel. They can be piped either using a plain tip or with a star tip, which gives the rings a pretty, fluted effect when baked. *Religieuse* are another popular type of filled dessert with a choux ring topped with a small cream puff, said to resemble nuns. Choux paste is really very versatile and can be formed into almost any shape you wish using a piping bag and tips, such as the choux hearts on page 50. I find that disposable piping bags are really useful for making choux pastries as most of the recipes in this book call for two or three piping bags.

This book contains all the classic choux recipes such as chocolate profiteroles with rich chocolate sauce and *Paris Brest*, filled with hazelnut praline and chocolate, and vanilla éclairs. The Fruity chapter has a wide variety of fruit-filled cream puffs, from amaretto and peach *Paris Brest* to blackcurrant éclairs. For more unusual, dainty recipes the Fancy chapter contains Earl Grey tea buns with delicate tea-flavored custard, rose and raspberry cream puffs, and violet éclairs. Finally, in the Dessert chapter, choux paste is used to make a variety of spectacular party treats such as *Gâteau St Honoré* on page 63 and an amazing *croquembouche* on page 60. These recipes take some time to prepare but are definitely worth the effort. Whatever flavor combination you prefer, there are recipes in this book that all will enjoy.

BASIC CHOUX PASTE

This basic choux recipe is used throughout the book. It needs a good strong arm and I find it is better beaten by hand than in a mixer as it is important to feel when the dough it ready.

Unlike pie or puff pastry, choux paste has a high moisture content as it contains water and lots of eggs. It is this moisture that causes the sticky dough to puff up into delicate pastry shells. It is important to measure your ingredients accurately and to sift as much air into the flour for best results. The dough can be made with water alone or a combination of water and milk to give a richer flavor.

Single quantity
$\frac{1}{2}$ cup all-purpose flour
3 tablespoons butter, cut into cubes
$\frac{1}{3}$ cup whole milk plus $\frac{1}{3}$ cup water
   or $\frac{2}{3}$ cup water only
1 teaspoon caster sugar
a pinch of salt
2 large eggs

Some of the recipes in this book call for more than one quantity of dough. Make in batches of no more than two quantities.

1 Sift the flour onto a sheet of baking parchment twice to remove any lumps and to add as much air as possible. (A)

2 Heat the butter in a saucepan with the milk and water (or just water if preferred), sugar and salt until the butter is melted. As soon

A

B

C

D

E

F

as the butter is melted remove the pan from the heat and quickly shoot in the sifted flour all in one go. It is important not to let the water heat for longer than it takes to melt the butter as this will evaporate some of the water and so there will be less liquid for the dough. (B)

3 Beat the mixture very hard with a wooden spoon or whisk until the dough forms a ball and no longer sticks to the sides of the pan and the pan is clean. At first the mixture will seem very wet but don't worry as it will come together after few minutes once the flour absorbs the water. It is important to really beat the mixture well at this stage. Let cool for about 5 minutes. (C)

4 Whisk the eggs in a separate bowl and then beat a small amount at a time into the dough using a wooden spoon or a balloon whisk. The mixture will form a sticky dough that holds its shape when you lift the whisk up. When you first add the eggs and begin beating the mixture will split slightly. This is normal and the dough will come back together as you continue to beat. The mixture must be beaten hard at each stage. (D) (E)

5 If the mixture is runny and does not hold its shape, unfortunately it cannot be used as it will not rise. Adding more flour to the mixture will not work. If this happens I tend to start again, although I have read that you can make a second batch of choux paste and add this wet mixture in, in place of the eggs and it will be rescued. (F)

Use the dough following the steps in each recipe.

PASTRY CREAM

Single quantity
1 egg and 1 egg yolk
1 heaping tablespoon cornstarch
5 tablespoons sugar
$\frac{2}{3}$ cup heavy cream
$\frac{1}{3}$ cup plus 1 tablespoon milk

Whisk the egg and egg yolk with the cornstarch and sugar until very thick and pale yellow in color. Place the cream and the milk in a saucepan and bring to the boil. Pour over the egg mixture, whisking all the time. Return to the pan and whisk over a gentle heat until the mixture becomes very thick. Pour into a bowl and let cool. Chill in the refrigerator until needed.

BASIC CHOUX PASTE **9**

CLASSIC

Chocolate éclairs, delicate pastries with vanilla filling, and topped with a rich chocolate ganache, are the most popular of cream puffs.

CLASSIC CHOCOLATE ÉCLAIRS
with pastry cream filling

1 quantity Basic Choux Paste
   (see page 8)

For the filling
1 quantity Pastry Cream
   (see page 9)
1 teaspoon vanilla bean
   paste (available online)
$\frac{2}{3}$ cup heavy cream

For the chocolate ganache
$6\frac{1}{2}$ oz dark chocolate
$\frac{1}{3}$ cup plus 1 tablespoon
   heavy cream
2 tablespoons butter
1 tablespoon golden
   syrup, light corn syrup
   or maple syrup

a baking sheet lined with
   baking parchment
   or a silicon mat
2 piping bags fitted with
   large plain tips
12 paper cases, to serve

Makes 12

Preheat the oven to 400°F (200°C) Gas 6. Spoon the choux paste into the piping bag and pipe 12 lengths of dough, about 4 inches long, onto the baking sheet, a small distance apart. Pat down any peaks in the dough using a clean wet finger. Sprinkle a little water into the bottom of the oven to create steam which will help the choux paste to rise. Bake in the oven for 10 minutes, then reduce the oven temperature to 350°F (180°C) Gas 4, and bake for a further 15–20 minutes until the éclair shells are crisp. Remove from the oven and using a sharp knife cut a small slit into each éclair to allow any steam to escape. Let cool.

Prepare the pastry cream for the filling following the method on page 9, adding the vanilla paste with the milk.

For the chocolate ganache topping, heat all the ingredients in a bowl over a pan of simmering water until melted. Dunk the top of each éclair into the ganache, then leave to set on a cooling rack.

When ready to serve, whisk the heavy cream to stiff peaks, and fold into the pastry cream. Spoon into a piping bag. Make a small hole in each éclair using a sharp knife and pipe until full.

Serve straight away or store in the refrigerator for up to two days.

COFFEE RELIGIEUSE

1 quantity Basic Choux Paste
(see page 8)

For the icing
2 cups confectioners'
sugar, sifted
3 tablespoons espresso coffee
12 coffee bean shaped
chocolates or decorations

For the filling
1 tablespoons instant coffee
granules
$1\frac{1}{2}$ cups heavy cream

For the buttercream
2 tablespoon salted butter,
softened
$1\frac{1}{3}$ cups confectioners'
sugar, sifted

*a large baking sheet lined
with baking parchment
or a silicon mat
3 piping bags, 2 fitted with
plain tips and 1 fitted
with a small star tip*

Makes 12

I love coffee cake in all of its forms and these delicate buns
are a firm favorite. With a strong coffee frosting and bitter coffee
filling these are a great pick-me-up treat.

Preheat the oven to 400°F (200°C) Gas 6.

Spoon the choux paste into a piping bag fitted with a plain tip and pipe
12 rings about 2 inches in diameter, and 12 small balls onto the baking sheets,
a small distance apart. Pat down any peaks in the dough using a clean wet finger.
Sprinkle a little water into the bottom of the oven to create steam which will help
the *religieuses* to rise. Bake in the oven for 10 minutes, then reduce the oven
temperature to 350°F (180°C) Gas 4, and bake for a further 15–20 minutes until
the pastries are crisp. Remove from the oven and using a sharp knife cut a small
slit into each of the rings and balls to allow any steam to escape. Let cool then make
a small hole in the bottom of each ring and ball ready for piping the filling in later.

For the icing, mix together the confectioners' sugar with the espresso coffee
until you have a smooth thick icing. Add the coffee gradually as you may not need
it all. Spread the icing over the tops of the rings and the balls. Place a chocolate coffee
bean or chocolate decoration on top of the balls and set aside for the icing to set.

For the filling, dissolve the coffee granules in 2 tablespoons of boiling water
and let cool. Pour half of this cooled coffee into a mixing bowl with the cream
and whisk to stiff peaks. Spoon into a piping bag fitted with a plain tip and
carefully pipe cream into each ring and ball, taking care not to touch the icing.
Pipe a small mound of cream into the center of each ring and place one of
the balls on top.

For the buttercream, whisk together the remaining coffee, butter,
and confectioners' sugar and whisk until light and creamy so that the
buttercream holds peaks when you pick up the whisk. Place into the piping
bag fitted with the small star tip and pipe pretty lines of decoration onto
the *religieuse* as shown in the photograph. Serve straight away or store
in the refrigerator until needed. The *religieuse* are best eaten on the
day they are made, although can be eaten the following day if stored
in the refrigerator.

These are a chocoholic's delight. Munching through the cocoa choux
pastry, chocolate ganache, white chocolate drizzle, and chocolate curls
prompted our village sewing circle to name them "Death by Chocolate"!

TRIPLE CHOCOLATE CREAM PUFFS

**1 quantity Basic Choux Paste
(see page 8 but follow
method here)**
4 teaspoons cocoa powder

For the chocolate glaze
$6\frac{1}{2}$ oz dark chocolate
**$\frac{1}{3}$ cup plus 1 tablespoon
heavy cream**
2 tablespoons butter
**1 tablespoon light corn
syrup or maple syrup**

To decorate
**$1\frac{1}{2}$ oz white chocolate,
melted**
chocolate curls

For the filling
$1\frac{1}{4}$ cups whipping cream

*2 piping bags fitted with
plain tips*
*2 large baking sheets lined
with baking parchment*

Makes 14

Preheat the oven to 400°F (200°C) Gas 6.

Make the choux paste as instructed on page 8, adding the cocoa powder
to the flour before sifting.

Spoon the chocolate choux paste into a piping bag and pipe 14 balls onto
the prepared baking sheets, a small distance apart. Using a clean, wet finger,
smooth down any peaks. Sprinkle a little water into the bottom of the oven
to create steam which will help the cream puffs to rise. Bake each sheet in the
oven for 10 minutes, then reduce the oven temperature to 350°F (180°C) Gas 4,
and bake for a further 15–20 minutes until the little puffs are crisp. Remove from
the oven and cut a slit into each puff to allow the steam to escape. Let cool then
make a small hole in the base of each puff for piping the filling in later.

For the chocolate glaze, put the chocolate, cream, butter, and syrup
in a heatproof bowl set over a pan of simmering water and simmer until
the chocolate has melted and the sauce is smooth and glossy.
Reserve a large tablespoon of the chocolate glaze for the
filling and let it cool. While still warm, dip the puffs into
the remaining glaze and place onto a cooling rack.
To decorate, dip a fork into the melted white chocolate
and drizzle thin lines of it over the buns. Sprinkle with
chocolate curls and allow to set.

When you are ready to serve, place the reserved
and cooled chocolate glaze with the whipping
cream in a bowl, and whisk to stiff peaks. Spoon
into a piping bag and pipe into each puff, through
the hole in the base. Serve immediately or store
in the refrigerator for up to two days.

VANILLA ÉCLAIRS
with Chantilly cream

1 quantity Basic Choux Paste
(see page 8)

For the icing & decoration
1 generous cup confectioners'
sugar, sifted
1 teaspoon pure vanilla extract
food coloring (optional)
sugar flowers
$\frac{1}{2}$ cup granulated sugar

For the Chantilly cream
seeds from $\frac{1}{2}$ vanilla bean
1 tablespoon confectioners'
sugar, sifted
$1\frac{1}{2}$ cups heavy cream

a large baking sheet, lined
with baking parchment
or a silicon mat
2 piping bags fitted with
plain tips

Makes 12

With origins in nineteenth-century France, the éclair remains one of the most popular pastries today. This version is filled with a classic Chantilly cream, sweet whipped cream with vanilla seeds.

Preheat the oven to 400°F (200°C) Gas 6. Spoon the choux paste into a piping bag and pipe 12 lengths of dough, about 4 inches long onto the baking sheet, a small distance apart. Pat down any peaks in the dough using a clean wet finger. Sprinkle a little water into the bottom of the oven to create steam which will help the éclairs to rise. Bake in the oven for 10 minutes, then reduce the oven temperature to 350°F (180°C) Gas 4, and bake for a further 15–20 minutes until the éclair shells are crisp. Remove from the oven and using a sharp knife cut a small slit into each éclair to allow steam to escape. Let cool.

For the icing, mix together the confectioners' sugar, vanilla extract, and 1–2 tablespoons of water until you have a smooth thick icing. Add 1–2 drops of food coloring of your choice, if desired, and mix. Spread the icing over the top of each éclair and decorate with sugar flowers. Set aside to set.

For the Chantilly cream, split the vanilla pod in half with a sharp knife and carefully remove the seeds with the back of a knife. Place the seeds, confectioners' sugar, and heavy cream in a mixing bowl and whisk to stiff peaks. Place into the second piping bag. Make a small hole in the underside of each éclair using a sharp knife and pipe cream into each until they are full.

To make the spun sugar, heat the caster sugar in a heavy based saucepan. Do not stir the sugar but swirl the pan to prevent the sugar from burning. The sugar will start to caramelize but you need to watch it carefully at this stage as it can very quickly turn dark and burn. Remove from the heat once melted to a golden colored caramel. Dip a fork into the sugar and pull it away from the pan to make long fine caramel strands. Immediately wrap each strand around a greased rolling pin to make sugar spirals. Serve immediately or store in the refrigerator for up to two days. The sugar work will become sticky over time so it is best to make the spirals just before serving.

18 CLASSIC

This delicacy of choux paste rings filled with praline cream was created in 1891 to celebrate the Paris—Brest—Paris bicycle race. Its classic shape was said to represent bicycle wheels.

PARIS BREST

1 quantity Basic Choux Paste
(see page 8)
3 tablespoons hazelnuts,
roasted, skinned,
and chopped

For the praline
$\frac{1}{2}$ cup sugar
$\frac{3}{4}$ cup hazelnuts, roasted,
skinned, and chopped

For the filling
$1\frac{1}{4}$ cups heavy cream
1 tablespoon hazelnut butter
confectioners' sugar, for
dusting

2 large baking sheets lined
with baking parchment
or silicon mats
2 piping bags, 1 fitted
with a round tip and
1 with a large star tip

Makes 9

Preheat the oven to 400°F (200°C) Gas 6. Spoon the choux paste into one of the piping bags and pipe 9 rings about 3 inches in diameter onto the baking sheets, a small distance apart. Pat down any peaks in the dough using a clean wet finger. Sprinkle the rings with the hazelnuts. Sprinkle a little water into the bottom of the oven to create steam which will help the rings rise. Bake in the oven for 10 minutes, then reduce the oven temperature to 350°F (180°C) Gas 4 and bake for a further 15–20 minutes until the pastry is crisp. Remove from the oven and cut a slit into each ring to allow any steam to escape. Let cool.

For the praline, heat the sugar in a saucepan until melted and golden brown. Do not stir the pan as the sugar is cooking but swirl it to ensure that the sugar does not burn. Spread the hazelnuts out on a greased baking sheet or silicon mat and carefully pour over the melted sugar. Let cool and then blitz in a blender to very fine crumbs.

For the filling, whisk together the cream and hazelnut butter in a mixing bowl to stiff peaks. Stir through the praline—or, if you do not have time to make the praline, substitute an extra tablespoon of hazelnut butter—with a spatula, reserving a little powder to sprinkle over the top of the rings.

Spoon the cream into the second piping bag fitted with the star tip. Carefully, cut each ring in half horizontally with a sharp knife. Pipe a swirl of cream into the bottom of each bun. Top each with the hazelnut covered rings and then dust with confectioners' sugar, sprinkle with a little of the praline powder, and serve immediately. These are best eaten on the day they are made, but can be eaten the following day if stored in the refrigerator.

CHOCOLATE PROFITEROLES

1 quantity Basic Choux Paste (see page 8)
1¼ cups whipping cream, whipped to stiff peaks

To serve with classic chocolate sauce
5½ oz dark chocolate (70% cocoa solids)
5 tablespoons butter
¼ cup heavy cream
3 tablespoons light corn syrup or maple syrup

To serve with fondue
8 oz dark chocolate
3½ oz white chocolate
⅓ cup almond liqueur or other liqueur of your choosing
⅔ cup heavy cream

2 baking sheets lined with baking parchment
2 piping bags fitted with plain tips
a fondue pot (optional)

Makes 25

Chocolate profiteroles are one of the most popular desserts. This recipe has two different sauces to choose from—a classic chocolate pouring sauce or a warm chocolate fondue to dip the profiteroles into.

Preheat the oven to 400°F (200°C) Gas 6.

Spoon the choux paste into one of the piping bags and pipe 25 small balls of dough onto the baking sheets, a small distance apart. Pat down any peaks in the dough using a clean wet finger. Sprinkle a little water into the bottom of the oven to create steam which will help the profiteroles rise. Bake in the oven for 10 minutes, then reduce the oven temperature to 350°F (180°C) Gas 4, and bake for a further 15–20 minutes until the profiteroles are crisp. Remove from the oven and cut a small slit into each puff to allow any steam to escape. Let cool.

When cool, spoon the whipped cream into a piping bag. Make a small hole in the base of each profiterole using a sharp knife and pipe cream in until each ball is full. Store in the refrigerator until you are ready to serve.

If serving the profiteroles with classic chocolate sauce, heat the chocolate, butter, cream, and syrup in a saucepan until the chocolate has melted and the sauce is smooth and glossy. Pour the warm sauce over the profiteroles to serve.

If serving the profiteroles with fondue, place the dark and white chocolates in a heatproof bowl set over a pan of simmering water, and add the almond liqueur and cream. Stir until the chocolate has melted and you have a thick chocolate sauce. Serve the sauce warm in a fondue pot with fondue forks for the profiteroles so that you can dunk them into the sauce.

The profiteroles are best eaten on the day they are made, although can be eaten the following day if stored in the refrigerator.

These tiny cream puffs are light and simple and although they contain no filling, with their crunchy sugar topping, they make a great mid-morning snack. It is best to make these buns with a milk dough as they are richer in flavor but you can replace the milk with water if you prefer. Pearl sugar is available from online baking stores. They have more sugar in than regular choux paste to improve the flavor and are also scented with vanilla.

CHOQUETTES

½ cup all-purpose flour
3 tablespoons plus 1 teaspoon unsalted butter, cut into cubes
⅓ cup water
⅓ cup milk
1 tablespoon granulated sugar
1 tablespoon vanilla bean paste (available online)
pinch of salt
2 large eggs
pearl sugar for sprinkling
plain chocolate chips (optional)

a piping bag fitted with a plain tip
2 large baking sheets lined with baking parchment or silicon mats

Makes 45

Sift the flour twice to remove any lumps. Heat the butter in a saucepan with the water, milk, sugar, vanilla bean paste, and salt until the butter is melted. Bring to the boil, then quickly add the sifted flour all in one go, and remove from the heat.

Beat hard with a wooden spoon or whisk until the dough forms a ball and no longer sticks to the sides of the pan. Let cool for about 5 minutes. Whisk the eggs and then beat into the pastry a small amount at a time using a wooden spoon or whisk. The mixture will form a sticky dough that holds its shape when you lift the whisk up.

Preheat the oven to 400°F (200°C) Gas 6.

Spoon the dough into the piping bag and pipe 45 small balls of dough a small distance apart on the sheets. Using a wet finger smooth down any peaks. Top the dough with sugar nibs. Sprinkle a little water into the bottom of the oven to create steam, which will help the choquettes rise.

Bake each sheet in the oven for 10 minutes, then reduce the oven temperature to 350°F (180°C) Gas 4, and bake for a further 10–15 minutes until the choquettes are crisp.

Remove from the oven and cut a small slit in each bun straight away to allow any steam to escape. Sprinkle a few chocolate chips over the warm buns, if desired. They will melt onto the puffs slightly for added indulgence. Serve the puffs warm or cold. The *choquettes* are best eaten on the day they are made but can be eaten the following day if stored in an airtight container.

These mini éclairs filled with coconut cream and topped with toasted coconut taste delicious. If you want to make them even more tropical you can add small pieces of pineapple to the éclair filling and add a little pineapple juice to the icing as well.

MINI COCONUT ÉCLAIRS

1 quantity Basic Choux Paste (see page 8)

For the filling
1¼ cups heavy cream
1 tablespoon coconut cream
1 tablespoon confectioners' sugar, sifted
1 tablespoon Malibu or other coconut liqueur

For the topping & icing
3 tablespoons coconut flakes
1½ cups confectioners' sugar, sifted
1 tablespoon coconut cream

2 baking sheets lined with baking parchment or silicon mats
2 piping bags fitted with plain tips

Makes 24

Preheat the oven to 400°F (200°C) Gas 6.

Spoon the choux paste into one of the piping bags and pipe 24 lengths of dough, about 1½ inches long onto the baking sheets, a small distance apart. Pat down any peaks in the dough using a clean wet finger. Sprinkle a little water into the bottom of the oven to create steam which will help the éclairs to rise.

Bake each sheet in the oven for 10 minutes, reduce the oven temperature to 350°F (180°C) Gas 4, and bake for a further 15–20 minutes until the éclairs are crisp. Remove from the oven and using a sharp knife cut a small slit into the sides of the éclairs to allow any steam to escape. Let cool. Make a hole in the base of each éclair ready for piping the filling in later.

For the filling, place the cream, coconut cream, confectioners' sugar, and Malibu in a bowl and whisk to stiff peaks. Spoon the cream into the other piping bag and pipe into each éclair through the holes you have made in the base. Store in the refrigerator until ready to serve.

Toast the coconut for the topping in a dry skillet until it starts to turn golden brown, stirring all the time. Watch carefully as it can burn very easily. Tip into a bowl and leave to cool.

For the icing, mix together the confectioners' sugar, coconut cream, and a little water until you have a thick icing. Spread the icing over the éclairs and sprinkle with the coconut. Serve as soon as the icing has set or store in the refrigerator until needed. The éclairs are best eaten on the day they are made, although can be eaten the following day if you wish.

FRUITY

Black currants always remind me of my Welsh grandparents as my Grandpa would grow them in abundance in his garden and my Gran would then use them to make the most delicious tarts. Both were excellent bakers and I am sure I inherited my love of baking from them. These éclairs are filled with juicy berries and have tangy black currant icing on top.

BLACK CURRANT ÉCLAIRS

1 quantity Basic Choux Paste (see page 8)

For the icing
$1\frac{1}{2}$ cups confectioners' sugar, sifted
1–2 tablespoons black currant syrup (see below)
$1\frac{1}{2}$ oz dark chocolate, melted

For the filling
$1\frac{1}{2}$ cups heavy cream
9.5 oz black currants preserved in light syrup, drained and syrup reserved

a large baking sheet, lined with baking parchment or a silicon mat
2 piping bags, 1 fitted with a large plain tip and 1 with a star tip
12 paper cases, to serve

Makes 12

Preheat the oven to 400°F (200°C) Gas 6.

Spoon the choux paste into the piping bag fitted with the plain tip and pipe 12 lengths of dough, about 4 inches long onto the baking sheet, a small distance apart. Pat down any peaks in the dough using a clean wet finger. Sprinkle a little water into the bottom of the oven to create steam which will help the éclairs to rise.

Bake in the oven for 10 minutes, then reduce the oven temperature to 350°F (180°C) Gas 4 and bake for a further 15–20 minutes until the éclair shells are crisp. Remove from the oven and cut a small slit into each éclair with a sharp knife to allow any steam to escape. Let cool.

For the icing, whisk together the confectioners' sugar with the black currant syrup until you have a smooth, thick icing. Spread over the top of the éclairs. Drizzle the melted chocolate over the éclairs in thin lines using a fork, then set aside for the icing to set.

When you are ready to serve, whisk the heavy cream and 3 tablespoons of the blackcurrant syrup to stiff peaks. Spoon into the piping bag fitted with the star tip. Carefully cut each éclair in half lengthways and pipe a swirled line of the cream into the bottom of each éclair. Place some of the black currants on top of the cream in each éclair. Cover with the iced tops and serve straight away or store in the refrigerator until needed. The éclairs are best eaten on the day they are made, although can be eaten the following day if you wish.

These éclairs are inspired by the elegant fresh fruit tarts that line the windows in French pâtisseries. They are simple to prepare and make a stunning addition to an afternoon tea cake stand.

FRESH FRUIT ÉCLAIRS

1 quantity Basic Choux Paste (see page 8)

For the filling
1¼ cups whipping cream, whipped to stiff peaks

For the topping
5 oz white chocolate
small pieces of fresh fruit of your choice (mango, grapes, raspberries and blueberries all work well)

2 piping bags fitted with plain tips
a large baking sheet lined with baking parchment or a silicon mat

Makes 12

Preheat the oven to 400°F (200°C) Gas 6. Spoon the choux paste into one of the piping bags and pipe 12 lengths of dough, about 4 inches in length onto the baking sheet, a small distance apart. Pat down any peaks in the dough using a clean wet finger. Sprinkle a little water into the bottom of the oven to create steam which will help the éclairs to rise. Bake in the oven for 10 minutes, then reduce the oven temperature to 350°F (180°C) Gas 4 and bake for a further 15–20 minutes until the pastry is crisp. Remove from the oven and cut a small slit into each éclair to allow any steam to escape. Let cool.

Working in a cool place as the éclairs need to be filled with the cream before being decorated as the decoration is fragile, make a small hole in the base of each éclair and pipe until full of cream.

For the topping, place the white chocolate in a bowl over a saucepan of water and simmer until the chocolate is melted. Leave for about 10 minutes so that the chocolate cools slightly and thickens. Using a knife, spread some white chocolate neatly over the top of each éclair. Place the small pieces fruit in decorative patterns on top of the chocolate. It is important to only use small pieces otherwise they will be too heavy and cause the éclairs to topple over. It is best to do this with the éclairs balanced in the grooves of a cooling rack.

Serve the éclairs straight away or store in the refrigerator until needed. The éclairs are best eaten on the day they are made, although can be eaten the following day if stored in the refrigerator.

These choux rings are topped with an almond crumble which gives a great crunchy texture to the choux. If you are serving to children simply omit the alcohol.

PEACHES & CREAM CHOUX RINGS
with Amaretti crumble topping

2 quantities Basic Choux Paste (see page 8)

For the crumble topping
4½ oz amaretti cookies or ratafia
1½ oz golden marzipan
3 tablespoons butter, melted

For the filling
2½ cups heavy cream
3 tablespoons almond liqueur
6 ripe peaches or nectarines
confectioners' sugar, for dusting

2 baking sheets lined with baking parchment or silicon mats
2 piping bags fitted with large star tips

Makes 18

Begin by making the crumble topping. Break the amaretti to very small pieces using your hands. Finely chop the marzipan and add with the warm melted butter to the amaretti pieces. Crush the mixture together with your hands until you have large crumbs of the mixture.

Preheat the oven to 400°F (200°C) Gas 6.

Spoon the choux paste into a piping bag and pipe 18 rings about 3 inches in diameter onto the baking sheets, a small distance apart. Pat down any peaks in the dough using a clean wet finger. Top each ring with a little of the crumble topping. Do not worry if any of the crumbs fall onto the sheet as these can be discarded after baking. Sprinkle a little water into the bottom of the oven to create steam which will help the rings to rise.

Bake each sheet in the oven for 10 minutes, then reduce the oven temperature to 350°F (180°C) Gas 4 and bake for a further 15–20 minutes until the rings are crisp. Watch that the crumble topping does not burn towards the end of cooking. Remove from the oven and cut a slit into each ring to allow any steam to escape. Let cool.

In a mixing bowl whisk together the cream and almond liqueur to stiff peaks. Cut the peaches or nectarines into thin slices, removing the pits. Spoon the cream into the second piping bag. Pipe a swirl of cream onto the buns. Top each with the fruit slices in pretty patterns and dust with confectioners' sugar to serve. Store in the refrigerator if not serving straight away as they contain fresh cream. These are best eaten on the day they are made.

CHERRY ALMOND PARIS BRESTS

1 quantity Basic Choux Paste (see page 8)

For the crumb mix
¼ cup self-rising flour
4 teaspoons butter
1 tablespoon granulated sugar
confectioners' sugar for dusting (optional)

For the filling
1 quantity Pastry Cream (see page 9 but follow method here)
1 teaspoon almond extract
⅓ cup plus 1 tablespoon heavy cream
10 oz (1¼ cups) cherry pie filling

a baking sheet lined with baking parchment
2 piping bags, 1 fitted with a plain tip and 1 with a star tip

Makes 12

These choux rings are topped with a crunchy buttery crumb mix and are filled with cherries and almond pastry cream. They are utterly delicious! You can replace the cherries with different pie fillings if you wish to make other fruit-filled choux. Apple pie filling with vanilla cream works very well.

For the crumb topping place the flour, butter and sugar in a bowl and rub together with your fingertips to fine crumbs. Set aside until needed.

Preheat the oven to 400°F (200°C) Gas 6.

Spoon the choux paste into one of the piping bags fitted with a plain tip and pipe 12 rings of dough onto the sheet. Pat down any peaks in the dough using a clean wet finger. Sprinkle over the crumb mix so that the top of each ring is covered lightly. Do not worry if any crumbs fall onto the sheet. These can be discarded after baking (or eaten!). Sprinkle a little water into the bottom of the oven to create steam which will help the pastries to rise.

Bake in the oven for 10 minutes, then reduce the oven temperature to 350°F (180°C) Gas 4 and bake for a further 10–15 minutes until the pastries are crisp and the crumb mix is golden brown. Remove from the oven and cut a small slit into each pastry to allow steam to escape. Let to cool.

Make the pastry cream following the instructions on page 9, adding the almond extract with the milk. Chill in the refrigerator until needed.

When you are ready to serve, whip the cream to stiff peaks then fold in the almond pastry cream. Spoon into the other piping bag fitted with a star tip. Cut each bun in half and fill with pastry cream and a spoonful of the cherry pie filling. Dust with confectioners' sugar to serve, if desired. Serve straight away or store in the refrigerator. These buns are best eaten on the day they are made, although can be eaten the following day if stored in the refrigerator.

Chocolate and passion fruit are a super modern combination—
the tanginess of the fruit brings the chocolate to life.

PASSION FRUIT ÉCLAIRS

**1 quantity Basic Choux Paste
(see page 8)**

For the mousse
**6½ oz dark chocolate,
melted**
**3 ripe passion fruit,
skins discarded**
**⅓ cup plus 1 tablespoon
heavy cream**
2 egg whites
**1½ tablespoons superfine
sugar**

For the icing & decoration
**1½ cups confectioners'
sugar, sifted**
**2–3 passion fruit, juiced
and seeds removed**
2 oz dark chocolate

*a baking sheet lined with
baking parchment*
*2 piping bags fitted with
large plain tips*

Makes 12

Begin by preparing the chocolate mousse as it needs time to set. Set the chocolate in a heatproof bowl set over a pan of simmering water until it is all melted. Stir the passion fruit juice, flesh and seeds, and heavy cream into the melted chocolate. The seeds of the passion fruit add a crunchy texture to these éclairs but if you are not keen on them, just remove them using a strainer and add the juice and flesh of the passion fruit to the chocolate mousse, leaving out the seeds. Whisk the egg whites to stiff peaks, then whisk in the superfine sugar gradually. Fold the egg whites into the chocolate and leave to chill in the refrigerator for about 3 hours or overnight until the mousse is set.

Preheat the oven to 400°F (200°C) Gas 6.

Spoon the choux paste into one of the piping bags and pipe 12 lines of dough onto the baking sheet about 4 inches in length, a small distance apart. Pat down any peaks in the dough using a clean wet finger. Sprinkle a little water into the bottom of the oven to create steam which will help the éclairs to rise.

Bake in the oven for 10 minutes, then reduce the oven temperature to 350°F (180°C) Gas 4 and bake for a further 15–20 minutes until the éclairs are crisp. Remove from the oven and cut a small slit into each pastry to allow steam to escape. Leave to cool then cut the éclairs in half lengthways.

For the icing, mix the confectioners' sugar with the passion fruit juice until you have a smooth icing, adding a little water if it is too stiff. This will depend on how much juice was released from your fruit so add gradually. Spread the icing over the tops of each éclair. Using a fork, drizzle thin lines of chocolate onto the icing and swirl in with a cocktail stick before the icing sets.

When you are ready to serve, spoon the choux pastry into the other piping bag and pipe a line of the chocolate passion fruit mousse into the bottom of each éclair. Cover with the iced tops and serve straight away or store in the refrigerator until needed. The éclairs are best eaten on the day they are made, although can be eaten the following day if you wish.

LEMON MERINGUE CREAM PUFFS

1 quantity Basic Choux Paste (see page 8)

For the lemon filling
6½ oz white chocolate
½ cup heavy cream
2 tablespoons prepared lemon curd
2 egg whites
2 tablespoons superfine sugar

For the icing
1⅓ cups confectioners' sugar, sifted
1 lemon, juiced
yellow food coloring

For the meringue topping
½ cup superfine sugar
1 tablespoon light corn syrup
¼ cup water
2 egg whites

a baking sheet lined with baking parchment
3 piping bags, 2 fitted with plain tips and 1 with a large star tip
a chef's blow torch

Makes 14

Taking inspiration from the classic lemon meringue pie, these dainty cream puffs have a creamy lemon filling and are topped with a sharp lemon icing and fluffy meringue.

Begin by preparing the lemon mousse as it needs to set before being used to fill the cream puffs. Melt the white chocolate in a heatproof bowl set over a saucepan of water, stirring occasionally. Once melted, remove from the heat and let cool slightly. Add the cream and lemon curd to the bowl and mix together to form a smooth paste. In a separate bowl, whisk the egg whites to stiff peaks. While still whisking, add the sugar gradually until the beaten whites are glossy. Gently fold the white chocolate mixture into the egg whites. Leave in the refrigerator to set, for at least 3 hours or preferably overnight.

Preheat the oven to 400°F (200°C) Gas 6. Spoon the choux paste into one of the piping bags fitted with a plain tip and pipe 14 balls onto the baking sheet, a small distance apart. Pat down any peaks in the dough using a clean wet finger. Sprinkle a little water into the bottom of the oven to create steam. Bake in the oven for 10 minutes, then reduce the oven temperature to 350°F (180°C) Gas 4 and bake for a further 15–20 minutes until the cream puffs are crisp. Remove from the oven and cut a small slit into each puff to allow steam to escape. Let cool then make a small hole in the base of each puff.

For the icing, mix together the confectioners' sugar with enough lemon juice until you have a smooth thick icing. Add a few drops of yellow food coloring if you wish. Dip the tops of the puffs into the icing, invert and leave on a rack to set.

For the meringue, heat the sugar, syrup and water in a saucepan and bring to the boil. Whisk the egg whites to stiff peaks and then pour the hot syrup into the eggs, whisking all the time. It is best to do this with a stand mixer or if you do not have one, have someone else pour the hot syrup in while you whisk. Whisk for about 5 minutes until the meringue is stiff and glossy.

Place the lemon mousse into the other piping bag fitted with a plain tip and pipe the mousse into each bun so that they are full. Spoon the meringue into the piping bag fitted with the star tip and pipe a large star of meringue on top of each bun. Using the blow torch, caramelize the meringue until lightly golden. The buns are best eaten on the day they are made.

These light cream puffs are inspired by the popular dessert apple strudel which contrasts the tangy apple perfectly.

STRUDEL CREAM PUFFS
with caramel glaze

2 quantities Basic Choux
    Paste (see page 8)

For the baked apples
4 large cooking apples
$4\frac{1}{2}$ cups sultanas
1 teaspoon ground
    cinnamon
3 tablespoons golden syrup
$\frac{1}{4}$ cup water

For the caramel glaze
$1\frac{1}{4}$ cups granulated sugar
1 tablespoon unsalted butter
pinch of salt
$\frac{1}{4}$ cup heavy cream
$1\frac{1}{2}$ cups confectioners'
    sugar, sifted

To assemble
$1\frac{1}{2}$ cups whipping cream,
    whipped to stiff peaks

an apple corer
2 baking sheets lined with
    baking parchment
2 piping bags, 1 fitted with
    a large plain tip and 1 with
    a large star tip

Makes 26

Preheat the oven to 350°F (180°C) Gas 4. Begin by preparing the apples as they need time to cool before being used to fill the cream puffs. Core the apples and using a sharp knife cut a slit horizontally around the apples. Place the apples in a roasting pan. Mix the sultanas with the cinnamon and fill the core of each apple with them. Spoon some golden syrup over the filled core of each apple and add the water to the dish. Bake the apples for 40 minutes then turn the temperature down to 300°F (150°C) Gas 2 and cook for a further 30 minutes. Remove from the oven and leave to cool. Discard the skins and mix the apple, sultanas and syrup together.

Preheat the oven to 400°F (200°C) Gas 6. Spoon the choux paste into the piping bag with a plain tip and pipe 26 balls of dough onto the baking sheets, a small distance apart. Pat down any peaks in the dough using a clean wet finger. Sprinkle a little water into the bottom of the oven to create steam. Bake each sheet in the oven for 10 minutes, then reduce the oven temperature to 350°F (180°C) Gas 4 and bake for a further 15–20 minutes until the cream puffs are crisp. Remove from the oven and cut a small slit into each bun to allow the steam to escape. Let cool.

For the caramel glaze, place the sugar, butter and salt in a saucepan and simmer over a gentle heat until the sugar and butter have melted and the caramel is golden brown. Remove from the heat and allow to cool for a few minutes then pour in the cream and whisk together until the caramel is smooth and glossy. Strain to remove any crystallized sugar and leave to cool. Mix the confectioners' sugar into the caramel sauce adding water if necessary then dip each bun into the glaze and leave on a rack to set.

When you are ready to serve, carefully cut each bun in half. Spoon the cream into the piping bag with a star tip and pipe a swirl of cream into the bottom of each bun. Top with a spoonful of the cooled apple. This will prevent the pastry becoming soggy from the apple. Top with the caramel glazed buns and serve straight away or store in the refrigerator until needed. The buns are best eaten on the day they are made.

FANCY

When raspberries are in season, these delicate choux rings are a perfect treat. With a rosy posy icing and crystallized rose petals, they make an elegant dessert bursting with tangy raspberries.

ROSE & RASPBERRY RINGS

1 quantity Basic Choux Paste (see page 8)

For the icing & decoration
1¼ cups confectioners' sugar, sifted
1 tablespoon rose syrup
pink food coloring
crystallized rose petals

For the filling
1¼ cups heavy cream
1 tablespoon rose syrup
10 oz raspberries

a large baking sheet, lined with baking parchment or a silicon mat
2 piping bags, 1 fitted with a plain tip and 1 with a star tip
10 paper cases, to serve

Makes 10

Preheat the oven to 400°F (200°C) Gas 6.

Spoon the choux paste into the piping bag fitted with a plain tip and pipe 10 rings of pastry, about 2½ inches in diameter onto the baking sheet, a small distance apart. Pat down any peaks in the dough using a clean wet finger. Sprinkle a little water into the bottom of the oven to create steam which will help the rings to rise.

Bake in the oven for 10 minutes, then reduce the oven temperature to 350°F (180°C) Gas 4, and bake for a further 15–20 minutes until the rings are crisp. Remove from the oven and cut a small slit into each ring to allow any steam to escape and let cool. Carefully cut each ring in half horizontally using a sharp knife.

For the icing, mix the confectioners' sugar with the rose syrup, and a few drops of food coloring until you have a thick icing, adding a little water if needed. Spread a little icing over the tops of the rings. Decorate each top with some crystallized rose petals and set aside for the icing to set.

Once the icing is set, whip the cream and rose syrup for the filling to stiff peaks then spoon into the piping bag fitted with a star tip. Pipe swirls of cream into the bottom of each ring. Top with fresh raspberries then place an iced ring on top of each one. Serve straight away or store in the refrigerator if you are not eating straight away. These cream puffs are best eaten on the day they are made.

VIOLET ÉCLAIRS

1 quantity Basic Choux Paste (see page 8)

For the icing
1 cup confectioners' sugar, sifted
1 tablespoon violet syrup or liqueur
purple food coloring

For the filling
1¼ cups heavy cream
1 tablespoon violet syrup or liqueur

To decorate
crystallized violets

a baking sheet lined with baking parchment
2 piping bags 1 fitted with a large plain tip and 1 with a star tip

Makes 12

These éclairs are inspired by the childhood sweet Parma Violets which my Grandma used to buy me when I was little. The flavor comes from violet liqueur or violet syrup, both of which are available online or in good delicatessens. If violet flowers are in bloom you can crystallize them yourself following the instructions on page 49.

Preheat the oven to 400°F (200°C) Gas 6.

Spoon the choux paste into the piping bag fitted with a plain tip and pipe 12 lengths of pastry, about 4 inches long onto the baking sheet, a small distance apart. Pat down any peaks in the dough using a clean wet finger. Sprinkle a little water into the bottom of the oven to create steam which will help the éclairs to rise. Bake in the oven for 10 minutes, then reduce the oven temperature to 350°F (180°C) Gas 4, and bake for a further 15–20 minutes until the éclair shells are crisp. Remove from the oven and cut a small slit into each éclair with a sharp knife. Let cool.

Carefully cut each pastry in half horizontally using a sharp knife. For the icing, whisk together the confectioners' sugar and violet syrup and a few drops of food coloring, if using, adding a few drops of water if necessary, and spread over the tops of the éclairs using a round-bladed knife. Decorate with the violets and let set.

For the filling, whisk together the cream and violet syrup (or liqueur) until the cream reaches stiff peaks. Spoon into the piping bag fitted with a star tip and carefully pipe a layer of cream into each éclair. Cover with the iced tops and serve straight away or store in the refrigerator until needed. The éclairs are best eaten on the day they are made, although can be eaten the following day if you wish.

Cooking with lavender from my garden is one of the things I like to do most. These profiteroles are served with a lavender syrup cream and are topped with a white chocolate sauce. Make sure that you use culinary lavender that has not been sprayed with any pesticides.

WHITE CHOCOLATE & LAVENDER PROFITEROLES

1 quantity Basic Choux Paste (see page 8)

For the filling
6½ tablespoons sugar
¼ cup water
1 teaspoon culinary lavender buds
1¼ cups heavy cream

For the sauce & decoration
6½ oz cream-filled white chocolate (such as Lindor White) or white chocolate
¾ cup plus 1 tablespoon heavy cream
1 tablespoon butter
purple edible glitter (optional)

2 baking sheets lined with baking parchment
2 piping bags fitted with large plain tips
a pestle and mortar
12–15 paper cases, to serve

Makes 25

Preheat the oven to 400°F (200°C) Gas 6. Spoon the choux paste into one of the piping bags and pipe 25 small balls of dough onto the sheets. Pat down any peaks in the dough using a clean wet finger. Sprinkle a little water into the bottom of the oven to create steam. Bake each sheet in the oven for 10 minutes, then reduce the oven temperature to 350°F (180°C) Gas 4 and bake for a further 10–20 minutes until the profiteroles are crisp. Remove from the oven and cut a small slit into each with a sharp knife to let any steam escape. Let cool.

Place the sugar and water into a saucepan and simmer until the sugar has dissolved, then bring to the boil. Grind the lavender using a pestle and mortar and add to the sugar syrup. Simmer for a minute then remove from the heat and let cool completely. When you are ready to serve whisk the heavy cream and lavender syrup together to stiff peaks. Make a small hole in the bottom of each profiterole, using a sharp knife. Spoon the cream into a piping bag and pipe into the profiteroles.

For the sauce, place the chocolate in a heatproof bowl set over a saucepan of water and simmer until the chocolate is melted. Add the cream and the butter and stir until melted. Coat the profiteroles and sprinkle with edible glitter, or serve with the sauce on the side either warm or cold. The profiteroles are best eaten on the day they are made, although can be eaten the following day if stored in the refrigerator.

PISTACHIO RELIGIEUSE

1 quantity Basic Choux Paste
(see page 8)

For the filling & decoration
¾ cup shelled pistachios
(unsalted)
2 tablespoons butter
2½ tablespoons
confectioners' sugar,
sifted
1⅔ cups heavy cream

For the icing
1¼ cups confectioners'
sugar, sifted
green food coloring

*a baking sheet lined with
baking parchment
3 piping bags, 2 fitted with
plain tips and 1
with a small star tip*

Makes 12

Pistachios are an exotic nut with a perfumed flavor. Good quality pistachios have a vibrant green color and when finely chopped make an elegant topping for these dainty *religieuse*.

Preheat the oven to 400°F (200°C) Gas 6.

Spoon the choux paste into a piping bag fitted with a plain tip and pipe 12 rings about 2 inches in diameter and 12 small balls of dough onto the sheet. Pat down any peaks in the pastry using a clean wet finger. Sprinkle a little water into the bottom of the oven to create steam which will help the choux pastry to rise.

Bake in the oven for 10 minutes, then reduce the oven temperature to 350°F (180°C) Gas 4, and bake for a further 15–20 minutes until the pastries are crisp. Remove from the oven and cut a small slit into each pastry to allow steam to escape. Let cool.

Reserve 12 whole pistachios for decoration, then blitz the remainder to very fine crumbs in a food processor or blender. Remove 3 tablespoons of the ground pistachios for decoration, then add the butter and confectioners' sugar to the blender, and blitz to a smooth paste to make pistachio butter. Whip the cream to stiff peaks. Remove a quarter of the cream and store in the fridge until you are ready to decorate. Make two small holes in the base of each ring, one on either side, and one small hole in each ball using a sharp knife. Fold the pistachio butter into the cream and spoon into a piping bag fitted with a plain tip. Pipe the cream into each ring and ball, piping through both holes on the ring to make sure that they are generously filled.

For the icing, mix the confectioners' sugar and food coloring with 1–2 tablespoons of cold water until you have a smooth thick icing. Spread some icing over each ring and sprinkle with the reserved chopped pistachios. Place one of the balls on top of each ring fixed in place with the icing and spread a little icing over the small balls. Place a whole pistachio in the center of each one. Spoon the reserved cream into the piping bag fitted with a small star tip and pipe small stars of cream onto the buns to decorate. Serve straight away or store in the refrigerator until needed. These are best eaten on the day they are made, although can be eaten the following day if you wish.

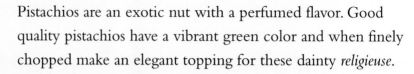

For a perfect afternoon tea why not serve these tea-infused
cream puffs topped with billowing sugar rose petals.

EARL GREY CREAM PUFFS

1 quantity Basic Choux Paste
(see page 8)

For the sugar rose petals
1 egg white
1 pesticide-free rose,
separated into petals
superfine sugar, for
sprinkling

For the pastry cream
$\frac{1}{4}$ cup boiling water
1 Earl Grey tea bag
1 quantity Pastry Cream
(see page 9 but follow
method here)

For the icing
1$\frac{1}{4}$ cups confectioners'
sugar, sifted
green food coloring

a clean small paint brush
a silicon mat
a large baking sheet lined
with baking parchment
or a silicon mat
2 piping bags fitted with
plain tips
12 paper cases, to serve

Makes 12 buns

Begin by preparing the sugar rose petals as they need to dry overnight. Be careful
to use roses which have not been sprayed with chemicals or pesticides. Whisk the
egg white until it is foamy. Paint a thin layer of egg white on both the front and
the back of a petal using the paint brush. Sprinkle it with superfine sugar. This
is best done by holding the superfine sugar at a small height above the petal and
sprinkling lightly. Have a plate below to catch any excess sugar. Repeat with all the
remaining petals and place on a silicon mat in a warm place to dry overnight.

For the Earl Grey pastry cream, pour the boiling water over the tea bag and
leave to steep for a few minutes. Remove the teabag. Make the pastry cream
following the instructions on page 9, adding the tea with the milk. Chill in the
refrigerator until needed.

Preheat the oven to 400°F (200°C) Gas 6. Spoon the choux paste into one
of the piping bags and pipe 12 large balls of dough onto the baking sheet, a small
distance apart. Pat down any peaks in the pastry using a clean wet finger. Sprinkle
a little water into the bottom of the oven to create steam which will help the
choux pastry to rise. Bake in the oven for 10 minutes, then reduce the oven
temperature to 350°F (180°C) Gas 4, and bake for a further 15–20 minutes until
the pastry is crisp. Remove from the oven and cut a small slit into each bun
to allow any steam to escape. Leave to cool.

Make a small hole in the side of each bun with a sharp knife. Spoon the pastry
cream into the other piping bag and fill each bun. Mix the icing to a stiff paste
with a little water and add the food coloring. Spoon the icing on
top of each bun and spread out using a round-bladed knife.
Place a rose petal on top and fix with a little icing.
Leave the icing to set and then serve straight
away placed in paper cases. The buns are
best eaten on the day they are made but can
be stored in the refrigerator and eaten the
following day if you wish.

HEART CREAM PUFFS

1 quantity Basic Choux Paste
   (see page 8)

For the sugar glaze
1½ cups confectioners'
   sugar, sifted
1 teaspoon vanilla extract
pink food coloring
sugar flowers, to decorate

For the marshmallow frosting
1¼ cups confectioners'
   sugar, sifted
1 tablespoon butter,
   softened
3 tablespoons marshmallow
   fluff
1 tablespoon milk

2 baking sheets lined with
   baking parchment
2 piping bags fitted with
   plain tips

Makes 14

If you want to treat a loved one or are having a special
Valentine's or wedding tea, then these hearts are perfect
to serve. They are filled with a rich marshmallow frosting
and topped with a sugary pink glaze. There can be no better
way to say "I Love You".

Preheat the oven to 400°F (200°C) Gas 6.

Spoon the choux paste into one of the piping bags and pipe 28 thin heart
shapes onto the baking sheets. Do not pipe the hearts too thickly or they will
lose their heart shape as they bake. Pat down any peaks in the dough using
a clean wet finger. Sprinkle a little water into the bottom of the oven to create
steam which will help the puffs rise.

Bake in the oven for 10 minutes, then reduce the oven temperature to
350°F (180°C) Gas 4, and bake for a further 5–10 minutes until the hearts are
crisp. Remove from the oven and cut a small slit into each heart to allow steam
to escape. Leave to cool.

For the glaze, mix the confectioners' sugar with 1–2 tablespoons of water,
the vanilla, and a few drops of pink food coloring until you have a runny icing.
Dip the tops of 14 hearts into the icing, invert, and place on a rack. It is best to
have a sheet of foil underneath to catch the icing drips. Decorate the iced hearts
with sugar flowers while the icing is still wet and set aside to set completely.

For the marshmallow frosting, whisk together the confectioners' sugar, butter,
marshmallow fluff, and milk until you have a smooth thick mixture. Spoon into
the other piping bag and pipe small blobs of frosting onto the un-iced hearts
following the shape of the heart. Place a decorated heart on top of each to serve.
The hearts are best eaten on the day they are made, although can be eaten the
following day if you wish.

These quirky cream puffs are filled with macadamia praline
custard and are topped with a Matcha green tea icing.

MACADAMIA & MATCHA CREAM PUFFS

**1 quantity Basic Choux Paste
(see page 8)**

For the macadamia filling
& decoration
**½ cup plus 1 tablespoon
granulated sugar
⅔ cup whole macadamia
nuts
1 egg and 2 egg yolks
1 tablespoon cornstarch
a scant ½ cup milk
1½ cups heavy cream**

For the icing
**1 teaspoon Matcha green
tea powder
1¼ cups confectioners'
sugar, sifted
green food coloring**

*a baking sheet lined
with baking parchment
or a silicon mat*
*2 piping bags fitted with
plain tips*
*a silicon mat or greased
baking sheet*
18 wooden skewers
18 paper cases, to serve

Makes 18

Preheat the oven to 400°F (200°C) Gas 6. Spoon the choux paste into one
of the piping bags and pipe 18 small balls of choux paste onto the baking sheets.
Pat down any peaks in the dough using a clean wet finger. Sprinkle a little water
into the bottom of the oven to create steam. Bake in the oven for 10 minutes,
then reduce the oven temperature to 350°F (180°C) Gas 4, and bake for a further
15–20 minutes until the cream puffs are crisp. Remove from the oven and cut
a small slit into each pastry with a sharp knife. Let cool then make a small hole
in the bottom of each puff using a sharp knife.

For the macadamia custard and decorations, first heat ½ cup granulated sugar
in a saucepan until it has melted. Leave to cool slightly until tacky then dip
18 individual nuts on wooden skewers into the caramel then hold upside down
until set. Place the remaining nuts on the silicon mat or baking sheet in a flat layer,
then pour the liquid caramel over the nuts, and leave to set. If your caramel
has cooled down simply return the pan to the heat for a few minutes until
runny. Once the layer of nuts have cooled, blitz in a blender to very fine
praline crumbs. In a separate bowl, whisk the egg and egg yolks with the
cornstarch and 1½ cups of sugar until very thick and pale yellow in color.
Place the milk and ⅔ cup of the cream in a saucepan and bring to the
boil. Pour over the egg mixture, whisking all the time. Return to the
pan and whisk over the heat until the mixture becomes very thick.

For the filling, whip a scant cup of the cream to stiff peaks then
fold in the macadamia custard and praline. Spoon into a piping bag
and pipe the custard into each bun through the hole in the bottom of each puff.

For the icing, mix the Matcha powder with a tablespoon of hot water and
make a paste. Add the Matcha paste to the confectioners' sugar and mix together
with a few drops of green food coloring and a little more water until you have
a smooth thick icing. Cover each puff with icing, place a nut on top, and let set.
The puffs are best eaten on the day they are made, as the caramelized nuts
will become sticky over time when they are exposed to the air.

DESSERT

Filled with sweet Chantilly cream, ripe strawberries and strawberry jam with an extra crunch of almonds, this is a perfect summer's day dessert. If you prefer you can pipe small rings and make individual desserts.

STRAWBERRY CREAM PUFF RING

2 quantities Basic Choux Paste (see page 8)
3 tablespoons flaked almonds

To assemble
2 cups heavy cream
1 tablespoon confectioners' sugar, sifted plus extra for dusting
1 teaspoon vanilla bean paste or pure vanilla extract (available online)
14 oz ripe strawberries
2–3 tablespoons strawberry jam

a baking sheet lined with baking parchment or a silicon mat
2 piping bags, 1 fitted with a large plain tip and 1 with a large star tip

Serves 8

Preheat the oven to 400°F (200°C) Gas 6.

Spoon the choux paste into the piping bag fitted with a plain tip and pipe large balls of the dough in a ring about 9 inches in diameter on the lined baking sheet. Pat down any peaks in the pastry using a clean wet finger. Sprinkle the top of the ring with the flaked almonds. Then sprinkle a little water into the bottom of the oven to create steam which will help the choux paste to rise.

Bake in the oven for 20 minutes, then reduce the oven temperature to 350°F (180°C) Gas 4 and bake for a further 25 minutes until the pastry is crisp. Remove from the oven and cut a few slits into the ring using a sharp knife to allow any steam to escape, then return to the oven for a further 5 minutes. Remove from the oven and leave to cool.

Once cool, cut the ring in half horizontally using a large serrated knife. The ring is fragile so you need to cut carefully. Do not worry too much if the top of the ring breaks as you can sandwich it back together with the cream filling.

Place the cream, confectioners' sugar, and vanilla bean paste in a mixing bowl and whisk to stiff peaks. Spoon the cream into the piping bag fitted with the star tip and pipe swirls of cream onto the bottom of each choux ball in the ring around the outside edge, reserving a little cream to decorate the top.

Reserve a few strawberries for decoration, then hull the remaining strawberries and cut into halves. Place the halved strawberries on top of the cream and top with small teaspoons of strawberry jam. Carefully set the almond-topped choux ring on top of the cream and strawberries. Dust with confectioners' sugar and then pipe small stars of cream on top of the ring before carefully placing the reserved strawberries on top.

Serve straight away or store in the refrigerator until needed. This is best eaten on the day it is made, although can be eaten the following day if you wish.

CARAMEL ALMOND PROFITEROLES

**1 quantity Basic Choux Paste
(see page 8)**
**3 tablespoons slivered
almonds**

For the filling
**1 heaping tablespoon
almond butter**
1 cup heavy cream

For the sauce
$\frac{1}{2}$ cup sugar
3 tablespoons butter
1 tablespoon almond liqueur
$\frac{1}{3}$ cup heavy cream

*2 baking sheets lined with
baking parchment
or silicon mats*
*2 piping bags fitted with
large plain tips*

Makes 25

These caramel profiteroles are topped with crunchy almonds
and filled with an almond cream, made with almond butter.
If you are not able to find almond butter then you can make
your own at home using the method below.

Preheat the oven to 400°F (200°C) Gas 6. Spoon the choux paste into one of
the piping bags and pipe 25 small balls of dough onto the baking sheets, a small
distance apart. Pat down any peaks in the dough using a clean wet finger. Sprinkle
the almonds over the top of the profiteroles, then sprinkle a little water into the
bottom of the oven to create steam which will help the choux to rise. Bake each
sheet in the oven for 10 minutes, then reduce the oven temperature to 350°F
(180°C) Gas 4 and bake for a further 15–20 minutes until the profiteroles are crisp.
Remove from the oven and cut a small slit into each bun with a sharp knife to
allow any steam to escape. Set aside to cool.

Place the almond butter in a bowl with the cream and whisk to stiff peaks.
Make a hole in the bottom of each bun with a sharp knife. Spoon the cream
into the other piping bag and pipe into each profiterole until they are full.

If you are not able to find almond butter, place $\frac{3}{4}$ cup of unsalted
blanched almonds in a blender with a tablespoon of confectioners' sugar
and blitz until they become a sticky paste. You may need to stop and scrape
the nuts down from the sides of the blender part way through blending.
Let the paste cool, as it will become hot during blending, before using.

For the sauce, heat the sugar and butter in a saucepan until the sugar
and butter have melted and start to caramelize. Cook over the heat until
the caramel starts to turn light golden brown, add the almond liqueur
to the pan and simmer for a further few minutes. Add the cream to
the pan, stir and remove from the heat.

Serve the buns straight away with the warm caramel sauce.
The profiteroles are best eaten on the day they are made, although
can be eaten the following day if stored in the refrigerator.

For a party or great after dinner dessert, why not serve these peppermint profiteroles filled with cold ice cream and topped with warm chocolate mint sauce. Garnished with mint leaves, these buns make the perfect end to any meal. If you wish you can crystallize the mint leaves following the instructions on page 49 for a pretty effect.

AFTER DINNER PROFITEROLES

1 quantity Basic Choux Paste (see page 8)

For the chocolate mint sauce
6 oz chocolate filled with mint fondant (such as Peppermint Patties)
$\frac{1}{2}$ cup heavy cream

For the filling
1 generous cup mint choc chip ice cream or other flavor of your choosing

To decorate
mint leaves

a baking sheet lined with baking parchment
2 piping bags fitted with large plain tips

Makes 16

Preheat the oven to 400°F (200°C) Gas 6. Spoon the choux paste into one of the piping bags and pipe 16 balls of dough onto the baking sheet, a small distance apart. Pat down any peaks in the pastry using a clean wet finger. Sprinkle a little water into the bottom of the oven. This will create steam which will help the choux pastry to rise. Bake in the oven for 10 minutes, then reduce the oven temperature to 350°F (180°C) Gas 4 and bake for a further 15–20 minutes until the profiteroles are crisp. Remove from the oven and cut a small slit into each profiterole to allow any steam to escape. Set aside to cool. Cut a small hole into the bottom of each bun with a sharp knife, ready for piping later.

For the chocolate mint sauce, place the chocolate mints and cream in a saucepan and simmer over a gentle heat until the mints have melted and the sauce is glossy.

Bring the ice cream to room temperature so that it is soft enough to pipe. Spoon into the other piping bag and working quickly pipe the ice cream into the buns. Serve straight away with the hot mint sauce and decorate with mint leaves. Alternatively you can freeze the filled buns for up to one month and defrost them slightly before serving, making the sauce at the time you wish to serve the profiteroles.

"*Croque en bouche*" after which this spectacular dessert is named literally translates as "crunch in the mouth" referring to the crack of the sugar coating when you bite into the profiteroles. This recipe creates a 16-inch tower but *croquembouche* can be made smaller (as photographed opposite).

CROQUEMBOUCHE

4 quantities Basic Choux Paste (see page 8)

For the filling
3 quantities Mousse (see page 35 and exclude the passion fruit)

To assemble
4 cups granulated sugar
sugar nibs and rice paper or sugar flowers, to decorate (optional)

4 baking sheets lined with baking parchment or silicon mats (or rewash and dry between use)
2 piping bags filled with plain tips
a large sheet of thin cardboard

Makes 80 profiteroles to serve 20–30 people

Begin by preparing the chocolate mousse as it needs time to set (see page 35).

Preheat the oven to 400°F (200°C) Gas 6. Spoon the choux paste into one of the piping bags and pipe about 80 small balls of pastry onto the sheets, a small distance apart. Using a clean wet finger smooth down any peaks. Sprinkle a little water into the bottom of the oven to create steam which will help the choux pastry to rise. Bake each sheet in the oven for 10 minutes, then reduce the oven temperature to 350°F (180°C) Gas 4 and bake for a further 10–15 minutes until the profiteroles are crisp. Remove from the oven and cut a slit into each profiterole to allow any steam to escape. Set aside to cool. Repeat with the remaining sheets until all the profiteroles are cooked. Once cooled, make a small hole in the base of each bun using a sharp knife.

Spoon the mousse into the other piping bag and pipe the chocolate mousse into each profiterole until they are full. Make a cone with the cardboard which is approximately 16 inches in height and 7 inches in diameter across the base, securing in place with adhesive tape. Place the cone in the center of a large cake stand.

In a heavy-bottomed saucepan, heat the granulated sugar until melted. It is best to do this in two saucepans, heating half the sugar in each. Do not stir the pan as the sugar is cooking but swirl it to ensure that the sugar does not burn. Once melted, carefully dip each bun into the caramel using tongs or your fingers but take extreme care as the sugar is very hot. Coat the profiteroles one at a time and place in a ring around the base of the cone. Repeat with all the remaining profiteroles, layer by layer, until the whole cone is covered. If you wish, dip the caramel coated profiteroles in sugar nibs for decoration. You need to work quickly before the sugar sets. If the sugar sets too quickly, just return it to the heat for a few minutes to melt it again. Once the whole tower is assembled, dip a fork into the remaining sugar and then spin it over the tower in thin lines to make spun sugar. Attach sugar flowers using a little of the sugar and serve straight away as the spun sugar will deteriorate and become sticky when exposed to the air.

This is a spectacular dessert for a special occasion, filled with roasted cinnamon plums and custard and topped with sugar-coated profiteroles.

GÂTEAU ST HONORÉ

2 quantities Basic Choux Paste (see page 8)

For the roasted plums
14 plums, halved and pitted
2 teaspoons ground cinnamon
1 tablespoon superfine sugar

For the filling
1¼ cups whipping cream, whipped
1 tablespoon confectioners' sugar, sifted
seeds of 1 vanilla bean

For the gateaux base
all-purpose flour, for dusting
1 pound puff pastry dough, thawed if frozen

For the caramel
& decoration
1 cup granulated sugar

2 baking sheets lined with baking parchment or silicon mats
an ovenproof roasting pan
3 piping bags, 2 fitted with plain tips and 1 with a star tip

Serves 12

Preheat the oven to 350°F (180°C) Gas 4. Place the plums, cinnamon and sugar in an ovenproof dish with a tablespoon or two of water and bake for about 20 minutes until the plums are just soft. Set aside to cool.

For a second time, preheat the oven to 400°F (200°C) Gas 6. On a flour-dusted surface, roll out the puff pastry dough thinly, then cut out a large circle about 11 inches in diameter. This is easiest done by cutting round a dinner plate. Prick the top of the pastry all over with a fork. Spoon the choux paste into a piping bag fitted with a plain tip and pipe a line of choux paste around the edge of the puff pastry and then a spiral in the center. Pipe the remaining choux paste into small round balls onto the other baking sheet. Pat down any peaks in the dough using a clean wet finger. Bake the puff pastry in the oven for 15 minutes, then reduce the oven temperature to 350°F and bake for a further 20–30 minutes until the pastry is crisp and golden brown. Repeat with the profiteroles, baking for 10 minutes at 400°F, then for a further 15–20 minutes at 350°F until the pastry is crisp. Remove from the oven and cut a slit into the profiteroles using a sharp knife. Leave to cool.

For the filling, whip the cream with the confectioners' sugar and vanilla seeds to stiff peaks, place into the piping bag fitted with a plain tip and fill each bun, reserving some cream for decoration. For the caramel, heat the granulated sugar in a heavy-based saucepan. Do not stir the sugar but swirl the pan to prevent the sugar from burning. The sugar will start to caramelize. Once the caramel is a golden color, remove from the heat. Using kitchen tongs dip the top of each profiterole into the caramel and then place in a ring around the edge of the puff pastry, fixing in place with a little cream and extra caramel if needed. If the caramel starts to set, return the pan to the heat for a further minute or so until it melts again.

Once the profiterole ring is in place, fill the centre cavity with custard, top with the roasted plums and then pipe the cream on top. To prepare the spun sugar decoration, reheat the caramel for a few minutes until the caramel is liquid. Leave to cool slightly then dip a fork into the sugar and pull it away from the pan to make long fine caramel strands. The spun sugar will melt when exposed to the air for a period of time so this needs to be served within a few hours of being decorated.

INDEX